Reading with Ricky
Mud, Turtles, and Tricksters

Stories by Kathy Kranking
Illustrations by Christian Slade

· ·

Contents

Rainy-Day Fun

Ricky Raccoon woke up one morning with a happy thought.

"Today is biking day!" he exclaimed. He was going to spend the whole day riding his new bike.

Ricky jumped out of bed. He ran to the door and pulled it open. Then he stopped and stared. "Oh, no!" he cried.

Big raindrops splashed into muddy puddles all over the ground. Everything was wet and drippy.

"I can't ride my bike in this weather!" Ricky grumbled. "Stupid rain. It's ruining everything."

"Hey, Ricky!" a voice called. It was Flora Skunk. She ran up quickly and ducked inside Ricky's house.

"I can't believe it's raining," she said, shaking her wet fur. "It's not exactly bike-riding weather."

"I know," Ricky said grumpily.

FLORA WONDERS

How was Ricky feeling when he saw it was raining?

3

"Well, that's OK," Flora said. "We can just stay inside and paint some pictures."

Ricky began to feel happier. He loved painting. "Good idea!" he said. Ricky and Flora got out the paints and began working. Ricky made a big, green oak tree. And Flora painted an orange kitty face.

Before long, Bizzie Beaver and Mitzi Mink poked their heads in Ricky's front door. "Hey, guys," Bizzie said, "why are you wasting a nice rainy day by staying inside?"

"Huh?" Ricky and Flora asked together.

"This is the time for some rainy-day fun," Mitzi said.

"But we ARE having rainy-day fun," said Flora. "We're painting."

BIZZIE ASKS

How was Ricky feeling when he was painting?

"No, we mean rainy-day fun out in the rain!" Bizzie said. "Come on—and bring your paintings!"

Rick and Flora looked at each other. "Why?" they asked.

Bizzie smiled mysteriously. "You'll see," he said.

The four friends headed outside. A nice, steady rain fell, with no thunder or lightning. "The ground is so soaked, it feels like a sponge!" Ricky exclaimed, jumping up and down.

"Lay the paintings on the ground," said Bizzie, "and watch what happens."

RICKY WONDERS

How did the paintings change in the rain?

Ricky and Flora put their paintings down. The rain fell *splat, splat, splat* onto them. After a few minutes, Ricky's oak tree began to look more like a weeping willow. Green drips ran down the painting like long, hanging branches. "Cool!" Ricky said. "My painting has turned into a RAINting."

Flora's kitty had changed, too. Now its fur looked longer. "If I use my imagination," she said, "it looks kind of like a lion with a mane."

"A lion with a mane that got caught in the rain," said Mitzi. Everyone laughed.

Ricky and Flora put their paintings back into Ricky's house to dry. Then they ran outside again.

"Time for more rainy-day fun," said Bizzie. He reached down and grabbed a pawful of mud. "Mud pies!"

Giggling with excitement, the friends picked up glops of mud and began shaping them into mud pies. "This is lots of fun!" Flora said. She squeezed the mud and watched it ooze between her fingers.

"We can make other shapes, too," said Ricky. "I'm making a mud man." He piled three mud balls on top of each other. Then he added some small pebbles and twigs.

Mitzi looked at her friends. "You know what?" she said. "We look like mud people, too!"

She was right. They were covered from head to toe with mud!

"You know," said Ricky, "I thought the rain was going to ruin the day. Instead, it made it more fun!"

Mud Lovers

Mud may be messy, but many animals love it.

An elephant calf loves to play in the mud.

A potter wasp collects mud and uses it to build its nest.

BIZZIE ASKS

Do you like mud?

A water buffalo uses dry, caked-on mud to keep bugs away.

The Lake Monster

Ricky Raccoon, Flora Skunk, and Bizzie Beaver were sitting on the shore of Clear Lake. Bizzie was tossing stones into the sparkling water.

"I'm tired of throwing stones," said Bizzie. "What else can we do?"

"Hmm," said Ricky. "We could go swimming."

"We just went swimming yesterday," said Flora.

"How about surfing?" asked Bizzie with a grin.

Flora giggled. "We'd need surfboards for that—and big waves."

BIZZIE WONDERS

What things would you like to do at a lake?

"Hey," said Ricky. "I know what we could do. We could build a raft out of fallen logs!"

"Let's do it!" said Flora. She and Bizzie began collecting logs. Ricky grabbed as many vines as he could find.

They lined the logs up next to each other, then used the vines to tie the logs together. As the friends stood back to admire their work, Sammy Skunk, Flora's little brother, came walking up.

"What are you doing?" Sammy asked.

"Look, Sammy," said Flora. "We built a raft." We're going to paddle around the lake on it. Want to come?"

Sammy looked at the raft. He looked out at the lake. Then he looked at the gang. "Um . . . what about the monster?" he asked.

Bizzie's eyes got big. "Monster? What monster?"

"The monster that lives in the lake," Sammy said. "I've heard a ton of stories about it."

Ricky grinned. "You can't believe everything you hear, Sammy. There's no monster," he said.

Flora patted Sammy's shoulder. "Don't worry," she said. "It will be fun!"

"Come on, let's see if our raft floats," said Ricky. Bizzie and Flora helped Ricky push the raft into the water as Sammy watched.

"It does!" said Bizzie. "Let's go!"

Flora splashed back to shore to grab a bag of snacks she had brought. Then she, Ricky, and Bizzie climbed aboard.

"Woo-hoo!" said Ricky. "All aboard who's coming aboard!"

"Come on, Sammy," said Flora.

RICKY WONDERS

Why didn't Sammy want to go on the raft?

Sammy wasn't sure what to do. The raft did look like fun. And there were snacks, too.

"Well, OK," he said. Sammy waded into the water and Flora pulled him onto the raft.

The friends used branches for oars. And as they paddled out into the lake, Sammy began to relax.

"This is fun," Sammy said. He reached for the snack bag and took a grape. Then he passed the bag to the others, and soon everyone was munching on grapes and enjoying the view.

Sammy took another grape and tried to toss it into his mouth, but he missed. The grape rolled off the raft and into the water.

"Oops," Sammy said, as he leaned out to grab the grape. But suddenly something lunged out of the water, right toward him!

"Aargh!" Sammy yelled. The others all shouted, too, and the raft rocked as everyone jumped in surprise.

Sammy scrambled away from the edge of the raft. He got to Flora and clung to her in fear.

"Let go, Sammy!" Flora said, trying to unwrap his arms from around her.

"It was the monster!" Sammy yelled. "It tried to eat me!"

Just then their friend Mrs. Cardinal landed on the edge of the raft. "What's going on here?" she asked. "I heard yelling."

"A scary monster tried to get me!" Sammy said.

"It looked like a big turtle," Ricky explained.

"Oh," said Mrs. C. "I think you must have met the snapping turtle. It lives in the lake."

"Told you!" said Sammy.

"Sammy," said Flora, "a turtle isn't a monster."

"Then why did it try to eat me?" Sammy asked.

"I think that snapping turtle was trying to eat the grape you dropped," said Bizzie, "not you."

"I didn't think of that," said Sammy.

"The turtle just wanted a snack," said Ricky.

"Well," said Sammy with a grin, "I'm glad that snack wasn't me!"

FLORA WONDERS

Was Sammy still afraid at the end of the story?

5 Things to Know About Snapping Turtles

1. **Their shells can be longer than rulers.**

2. **They have long tails.**

3. **They will eat anything they can find.**

4. **They live by themselves in shallow water.**

5. **They do not attack people when they are in the water.**

The Tricksters

Ricky Raccoon was making himself a cup of cocoa. He put in chocolate, sugar, and warm milk. Then he mixed it all up. He took a sip, expecting the taste of sweet chocolate. But instead, he tasted salt.

"Yuck!" Ricky exclaimed. "What is salt doing in my cocoa?"

Ricky looked into the sugar jar. Then he dabbed a little on his paw and tasted it.

"Ugh!" he said. "This isn't sugar. It's salt. Why is salt in my sugar jar? I know—this must be the work of Bizzie Beaver!"

Ricky and Bizzie had been playing tricks on each other all week.

"That's OK," Ricky said to himself. "I'll get him back."

RICKY WONDERS

Has someone ever played a trick on you?

Later that day, Bizzie came out of his stick lodge onto the shore of the pond. On his picnic table he saw a bright red apple. "Mmm," said Bizzie. "I wonder who left me this apple."

Bizzie picked up the apple and was about to take a bite out of it. Then suddenly he shouted and dropped it. "Yuck, there's a worm in the apple!" he said. "That's gross!"

But then he looked closer. There was something funny about the worm. Suddenly Bizzie laughed. The worm poking out of a hole in the apple was a gummy worm!

"Very funny, Ricky, wherever you are," Bizzie said.

As the week went on, the tricks continued. One day Bizzie found a pretty rock next to the leg of his picnic table. "Oh, that would be a nice rock for my collection," he said. But when he tried to pick it up, he found it had been glued to the table leg! "Ricky strikes again," Bizzie said.

FLORA WANTS TO KNOW

What tricks have you played on your friends?

The next morning, Ricky couldn't find his cap. "That's funny," he said. Capless, Ricky headed outside. He walked along the path a short distance, then noticed something ahead.

"My cap!" Ricky said in surprise. "I wonder how it got out here in the woods." He hurried over to the cap and bent to pick it up. But as he did, the cap moved out of the way!

"What's going on?" Ricky asked. He reached for the cap again. And again the cap moved! Then Ricky noticed a string attached to the cap.

"Ah-ha!" said Ricky. He took the string off the cap and put the cap on his head. "I think I know who's at the other end of this string!" he said. Ricky began following the string until it disappeared behind a bush.

Ricky ran behind the bush to where Bizzie was crouched down, hiding. "Gotcha!" Ricky shouted.

Bizzie ran away giggling and Ricky took off after him. The two friends ran along the path, laughing and yelling, until suddenly Bizzie screeched to a stop and Ricky ran into him.

"Look!" said Bizzie. There, lying on the ground, was an opossum. Its eyes were closed and its mouth was open.

"Uh-oh," said Ricky.

"What do you think is wrong with it?" asked Bizzie.

Just then, their friend Mrs. Cardinal landed on a nearby branch. "Hello, boys," she said.

"Mrs. C, look! Something's wrong with this opossum," said Ricky.

"It looks like it's dead!" Bizzie added.

Mrs. C smiled. "Don't worry," she replied. "The opossum isn't dead. It is just playing dead."

"Huh?" asked Ricky.

"Well," said Mrs. C, "if something scares an opossum enough, it kind of faints. That way it can fool an enemy into thinking it's dead. Then maybe it will leave the opossum alone."

"I guess the opossum got scared when it heard us coming down the path," said Ricky.

BIZZIE ASKS

How did it help the opossum to pretend it was dead?

"Hey, let's hide for a while and see if it wakes up," said Bizzie.

So the three of them hid in the bushes and watched. Sure enough, after a few minutes, the opossum began to move. It stood up and shook itself. Then it wandered away.

"Well, what do you know," said Ricky. "It looks like we're not the only tricksters in the woods!"

Animal Tricksters

Meet another animal that plays dead to stay safe.

Grass Snake

A grass snake rolls over and pretends to be dead when an enemy is nearby. Most animals fall for the bluff and walk away, thinking the animal is really dead.

31

Published by the National Wildlife Federation.

"Ricky and Pals" originally appeared in RANGER RICK JR, a publication for children ages 4–7 in the Ranger Rick family of magazines.

Kathy Kranking, Author
Christian Slade, Illustrator
Molly Woods, Reading Consultant

Photo and Illustration Credits:
Page 10: Gerry Ellis / Minden Pictures; Page 11: Natasha Mhatre (top), Martin Harvey / DRK Photo (bottom); Page 21: George Sanker / NPL / Minden Pictures; Page 31: Stephen Dalton / Minden Pictures.

Printed in the United States of America.

RangerRick.org

ISBN: 978-1-947254-26-8